Days Gone By
Weekly Planner for the Vintage Heart

Activinotes

Activinotes
DAILY JOURNALS, PLANNERS, NOTEBOOKS AND OTHER BLANK BOOKS

Weekly Planner

MONDAY	TUESDAY	WEDNESDAY	To Do List

THURSDAY	FRIDAY	SATURDAY	To Buy List

SUNDAY	To Do List

Notes *and*
Reminders

Weekly Planner

MONDAY	TUESDAY	WEDNESDAY	To Do List

THURSDAY	FRIDAY	SATURDAY	To Buy List

SUNDAY		To Do List

Notes *and*
Reminders

Weekly Planner

MONDAY	TUESDAY	WEDNESDAY	To Do List

THURSDAY	FRIDAY	SATURDAY	To Buy List

SUNDAY	To Do List

Notes *and*
Reminders

Weekly Planner

MONDAY	TUESDAY	WEDNESDAY	To Do List

THURSDAY	FRIDAY	SATURDAY	To Buy List

SUNDAY	To Do List

Notes and
Reminders

Weekly Planner

MONDAY	TUESDAY	WEDNESDAY	To Do List

THURSDAY	FRIDAY	SATURDAY	To Buy List

SUNDAY			To Do List

Notes and
Reminders

Weekly Planner

MONDAY	TUESDAY	WEDNESDAY	To Do List

THURSDAY	FRIDAY	SATURDAY	To Buy List

SUNDAY			To Do List

Notes *and*
Reminders

Weekly Planner

MONDAY	TUESDAY	WEDNESDAY	To Do List

THURSDAY	FRIDAY	SATURDAY	To Buy List

SUNDAY	To Do List

Notes *and*
Reminders

Weekly Planner

MONDAY	TUESDAY	WEDNESDAY	To Do List

THURSDAY	FRIDAY	SATURDAY	To Buy List

SUNDAY	To Do List

Notes and
Reminders

Weekly Planner

MONDAY	TUESDAY	WEDNESDAY	To Do List

THURSDAY	FRIDAY	SATURDAY	To Buy List

SUNDAY			To Do List

Notes and
Reminders

Weekly Planner

MONDAY	TUESDAY	WEDNESDAY	To Do List

THURSDAY	FRIDAY	SATURDAY	To Buy List

SUNDAY	To Do List

Notes and
Reminders

Weekly Planner

MONDAY	TUESDAY	WEDNESDAY	To Do List

THURSDAY	FRIDAY	SATURDAY	To Buy List

SUNDAY	To Do List

Notes *and*
Reminders

Weekly Planner

MONDAY	TUESDAY	WEDNESDAY	To Do List

THURSDAY	FRIDAY	SATURDAY	To Buy List

SUNDAY		To Do List

Notes and
Reminders

Weekly Planner

MONDAY	TUESDAY	WEDNESDAY	To Do List

THURSDAY	FRIDAY	SATURDAY	To Buy List

SUNDAY			To Do List

Notes *and*
Reminders

Weekly Planner

MONDAY	TUESDAY	WEDNESDAY	To Do List

THURSDAY	FRIDAY	SATURDAY	To Buy List

SUNDAY			To Do List

Notes and Reminders

Weekly Planner

MONDAY	TUESDAY	WEDNESDAY	To Do List

THURSDAY	FRIDAY	SATURDAY	To Buy List

SUNDAY			To Do List

Notes and
Reminders

Weekly Planner

MONDAY	TUESDAY	WEDNESDAY	To Do List

THURSDAY	FRIDAY	SATURDAY	To Buy List

SUNDAY			To Do List

Notes and
Reminders

Weekly Planner

MONDAY	TUESDAY	WEDNESDAY	To Do List

THURSDAY	FRIDAY	SATURDAY	To Buy List

SUNDAY	To Do List

Notes *and*
Reminders

Weekly Planner

MONDAY	TUESDAY	WEDNESDAY	To Do List

THURSDAY	FRIDAY	SATURDAY	To Buy List

SUNDAY		To Do List

Notes *and* Reminders

Weekly Planner

MONDAY	TUESDAY	WEDNESDAY	To Do List

THURSDAY	FRIDAY	SATURDAY	To Buy List

SUNDAY	To Do List

Notes *and*
Reminders

Weekly Planner

MONDAY	TUESDAY	WEDNESDAY	To Do List

THURSDAY	FRIDAY	SATURDAY	To Buy List

SUNDAY			To Do List

Notes and
Reminders

Weekly Planner

MONDAY	TUESDAY	WEDNESDAY	To Do List

THURSDAY	FRIDAY	SATURDAY	To Buy List

SUNDAY			To Do List

Notes and
Reminders

Weekly Planner

MONDAY	TUESDAY	WEDNESDAY	To Do List

THURSDAY	FRIDAY	SATURDAY	To Buy List

SUNDAY			To Do List

Notes and
Reminders

Weekly Planner

MONDAY	TUESDAY	WEDNESDAY	To Do List

THURSDAY	FRIDAY	SATURDAY	To Buy List

SUNDAY	To Do List

Notes and
Reminders

Weekly Planner

MONDAY	TUESDAY	WEDNESDAY	To Do List

THURSDAY	FRIDAY	SATURDAY	To Buy List

SUNDAY	To Do List

Notes *and*
Reminders

Weekly Planner

MONDAY	TUESDAY	WEDNESDAY	To Do List

THURSDAY	FRIDAY	SATURDAY	To Buy List

SUNDAY	To Do List

Notes and
Reminders

Weekly Planner

MONDAY	TUESDAY	WEDNESDAY	To Do List

THURSDAY	FRIDAY	SATURDAY	To Buy List

SUNDAY		To Do List

Notes and
Reminders

Weekly Planner

MONDAY	TUESDAY	WEDNESDAY	To Do List

THURSDAY	FRIDAY	SATURDAY	To Buy List

SUNDAY			To Do List

Notes and *Reminders*

Weekly Planner

MONDAY	TUESDAY	WEDNESDAY	To Do List

THURSDAY	FRIDAY	SATURDAY	To Buy List

SUNDAY		To Do List

Notes and
Reminders

Weekly Planner

MONDAY	TUESDAY	WEDNESDAY	To Do List

THURSDAY	FRIDAY	SATURDAY	To Buy List

SUNDAY	To Do List

Notes *and*
Reminders

Weekly Planner

MONDAY	TUESDAY	WEDNESDAY	To Do List

THURSDAY	FRIDAY	SATURDAY	To Buy List

SUNDAY		To Do List

Notes and
Reminders

Weekly Planner

MONDAY	TUESDAY	WEDNESDAY	To Do List

THURSDAY	FRIDAY	SATURDAY	To Buy List

SUNDAY			To Do List

Notes and
Reminders

Weekly Planner

MONDAY	TUESDAY	WEDNESDAY	To Do List

THURSDAY	FRIDAY	SATURDAY	To Buy List

SUNDAY		To Do List

Notes *and*
Reminders

Weekly Planner

MONDAY	TUESDAY	WEDNESDAY	To Do List

THURSDAY	FRIDAY	SATURDAY	To Buy List

SUNDAY	To Do List

Notes and
Reminders

Weekly Planner

MONDAY	TUESDAY	WEDNESDAY	To Do List

THURSDAY	FRIDAY	SATURDAY	To Buy List

SUNDAY			To Do List

Notes and
Reminders

Weekly Planner

MONDAY	TUESDAY	WEDNESDAY	To Do List

THURSDAY	FRIDAY	SATURDAY	To Buy List

SUNDAY			To Do List

Notes *and*
Reminders

Weekly Planner

MONDAY	TUESDAY	WEDNESDAY	To Do List

THURSDAY	FRIDAY	SATURDAY	To Buy List

SUNDAY	To Do List

Notes and
Reminders

Weekly Planner

MONDAY	TUESDAY	WEDNESDAY	To Do List

THURSDAY	FRIDAY	SATURDAY	To Buy List

SUNDAY			To Do List

Notes and
Reminders

Weekly Planner

MONDAY	TUESDAY	WEDNESDAY	To Do List

THURSDAY	FRIDAY	SATURDAY	To Buy List

SUNDAY		To Do List

Notes *and*
Reminders

Weekly Planner

MONDAY	TUESDAY	WEDNESDAY	To Do List

THURSDAY	FRIDAY	SATURDAY	To Buy List

SUNDAY	To Do List

Notes and
Reminders

Weekly Planner

MONDAY	TUESDAY	WEDNESDAY	To Do List

THURSDAY	FRIDAY	SATURDAY	To Buy List

SUNDAY			To Do List

Notes and
Reminders

Weekly Planner

MONDAY	TUESDAY	WEDNESDAY	To Do List

THURSDAY	FRIDAY	SATURDAY	To Buy List

SUNDAY			To Do List

Notes and Reminders

Weekly Planner

MONDAY	TUESDAY	WEDNESDAY	To Do List

THURSDAY	FRIDAY	SATURDAY	To Buy List

SUNDAY	To Do List

Notes *and*
Reminders

Weekly Planner

MONDAY	TUESDAY	WEDNESDAY	To Do List

THURSDAY	FRIDAY	SATURDAY	To Buy List

SUNDAY		To Do List

Notes and
Reminders

Weekly Planner

MONDAY	TUESDAY	WEDNESDAY	To Do List

THURSDAY	FRIDAY	SATURDAY	To Buy List

SUNDAY	To Do List

Notes and
Reminders

Weekly Planner

MONDAY	TUESDAY	WEDNESDAY	To Do List

THURSDAY	FRIDAY	SATURDAY	To Buy List

SUNDAY			To Do List

Notes and
Reminders

Weekly Planner

MONDAY	TUESDAY	WEDNESDAY	To Do List

THURSDAY	FRIDAY	SATURDAY	To Buy List

SUNDAY	To Do List

Notes and
Reminders

Weekly Planner

MONDAY	TUESDAY	WEDNESDAY	To Do List

THURSDAY	FRIDAY	SATURDAY	To Buy List

SUNDAY		To Do List

Notes and
Reminders

Weekly Planner

MONDAY	TUESDAY	WEDNESDAY	To Do List

THURSDAY	FRIDAY	SATURDAY	To Buy List

SUNDAY		To Do List

Notes *and*
Reminders

Weekly Planner

MONDAY	TUESDAY	WEDNESDAY	To Do List

THURSDAY	FRIDAY	SATURDAY	To Buy List

SUNDAY	To Do List

Notes and Reminders

Weekly Planner

MONDAY	TUESDAY	WEDNESDAY	To Do List

THURSDAY	FRIDAY	SATURDAY	To Buy List

SUNDAY	To Do List

Notes *and*
Reminders

Weekly Planner

MONDAY	TUESDAY	WEDNESDAY	To Do List

THURSDAY	FRIDAY	SATURDAY	To Buy List

SUNDAY	To Do List

Notes *and*
Reminders

Notes

www.ingramcontent.com/pod-product-compliance
Lightning Source LLC
Chambersburg PA
CBHW081333090426
42737CB00017B/3131